FOLLOWING A FAITH

A Muslim life

Cath Senker

PowerKiDS
press™

Published in 2020 by **The Rosen Publishing Group, Inc.**
29 East 21st Street, New York, NY 10010

Cataloging-in-Publication Data

Names: Senker, Cath.
Title: A Muslim life / Cath Senker.
Description: New York : PowerKids Press, 2020. | Series: Following a faith |
Includes glossary and index.
Identifiers: ISBN 9781725303577 (pbk.) | ISBN 9781725303591 (library bound) |
ISBN 9781725303584 (6pack)
Subjects: LCSH: Islam--Juvenile literature. | Fasts and feasts--Islam--Juvenile
literature. | Islam--Customs and practices--Juvenile literature.
Classification: LCC BP161.3 S46 2020 | DDC 297--dc23

Credits
Series Editor: Amy Pimperton/Julia Bird
Series Designer: Krina Patel

Picture credits: Anadolu Agency/Getty Images: 19t. Arne9001/Dreamstime: 9br.
Art Directors & Trip/Alamy: 25b. Muhammad Bazuki /Reuters: 7. Youssef Boudial/
Reuters: 17b. Pavlos Christoforou/Alamy: 9t. Creativa Images/Shutterstock: 9bl.
Curioso/Shutterstock: front cover main. Distinctive Images/Shutterstock: 11t.
Donyanedomam/Dreamstime: 15b. Egyptian Studio/Shutterstock: 5t. S Forster/Alamy:
10. Fotoflirt/Alamy: 25t. Paul Gapper/Alamy: 22. Godong/Alamy 19b. Godong/
Robert Harding PL: 28. Sadik Gulec/Dreamstime: 17t. Ramzi Hachicho/Dreamstime:
27. Atef Hassan/Reuters: 16. Faisal Idris/Dreamstime: 21bl. Mohammad Saiful Islam/
Shutterstock: 1, 15t. Javarman/Dreamstime: 14 main. Trevor Kittelty/Shutterstock:
14 inset. Lucid Waters/Dreamstime: 23t. Jeff Morgan15/Alamy: 18. Juan Moyano/
Dreamstime: 17c. Christine Osborne/World Religions PL/Alamy: 6. Altin Osmanaj/
Shutterstock: 24. Pniesen/Dreamstime: 20. Wigbert Roth/imagebroker/Superstock: 8.
Suhaid Salem/Reuters: 26. Shamleen/Shutterstock: 29t. Tokjanggut/Dreamstime: 4.
Vector Painter/Shutterstock: front cover c. Visuals Stock/Alamy: 5b. Janine Wiedel/
Alamy: 11b. Gregory Wrona/Alamy: 12. Altaf Zargar/Zuma Press/Alamy: 21br. Zuma
Press/Alamy: 23b. Zurijeta/Shutterstock: 13, 29br.

Manufactured in the United States of America

CPSIA Compliance Information: Batch CSPK19: For Further Information contact Rosen Publishing,
New York, New York at 1-800-237-9932.

CONTENTS

WHAT DOES IT MEAN TO BE A MUSLIM?

Muslims follow the faith of Islam. They believe in one God, Allah, and his final messenger, the Prophet Muhammad. Born in Mecca, Arabia, in AD 570, Muhammad was a spiritual man. It is believed Allah revealed his messages to him, and Allah's words were written down in beautiful Arabic prose to form the book of the holy Qur'an.

ONE COMMUNITY

The Qur'an explains that people should live united as one community: "Mankind. We created you from a single pair of a male and a female, and made you into nations and tribes, that you may know each other."
(Qur'an 49:13)

THE UMMAH

Muslims are part of a worldwide community of more than 1.5 billion people – the *ummah*. Anyone can become a Muslim if they choose to; people of all races and from many countries are Muslims. Praying together and gathering at the mosque help Muslims to feel part of the ummah and closer to Allah.

The Qur'an is the holy book of the Islamic faith. Many are beautifully decorated.

A GOOD LIFE

The Prophet Muhammad taught the wisdom of the Qur'an: tolerance, respect, and kindness to other people. Muslims follow his example and the guidance in their holy book for leading a good life. For example, children should offer respect to their parents and never tell lies.

ALLAH

Being a Muslim is about how you live your life, not just following the customs: "If you want to focus more on Allah in your prayers, focus more on Him outside your prayers."
- Yasmin Mogahed

PRAYER

Praying five times a day is an essential part of being a Muslim. Muslims are encouraged to pray together in a mosque, but if they cannot, then they can pray at home, school, work, or wherever they are.

Prayer times vary according to the position of the sun, so they change throughout the year.

BORN INTO THE MUSLIM FAITH

To Muslims, a baby is a gift from Allah and brings *barakah* – blessings. Families wish to bring up their children with the beliefs of their faith from the very beginning.

FIRST WORDS

The first words a new baby should hear are "*Allahu Akbar*" ("God is greatest"). Before the baby is washed and dressed, the father says the *adhan*, the call to prayer that invites worshippers to the mosque. He whispers the prayer in the baby's right ear, followed by the *iqamah* prayer in the left ear – the prayer offered at the start of worship in the mosque.

TAHNIK CEREMONY

Now, a little date juice or honey is placed on the baby's tongue. The honey is a symbol. It is given so that the baby's first taste of life should be sweet, and the taste is linked to the sweet words of the Qur'an. It is also hoped it will make the baby sweet-tempered!

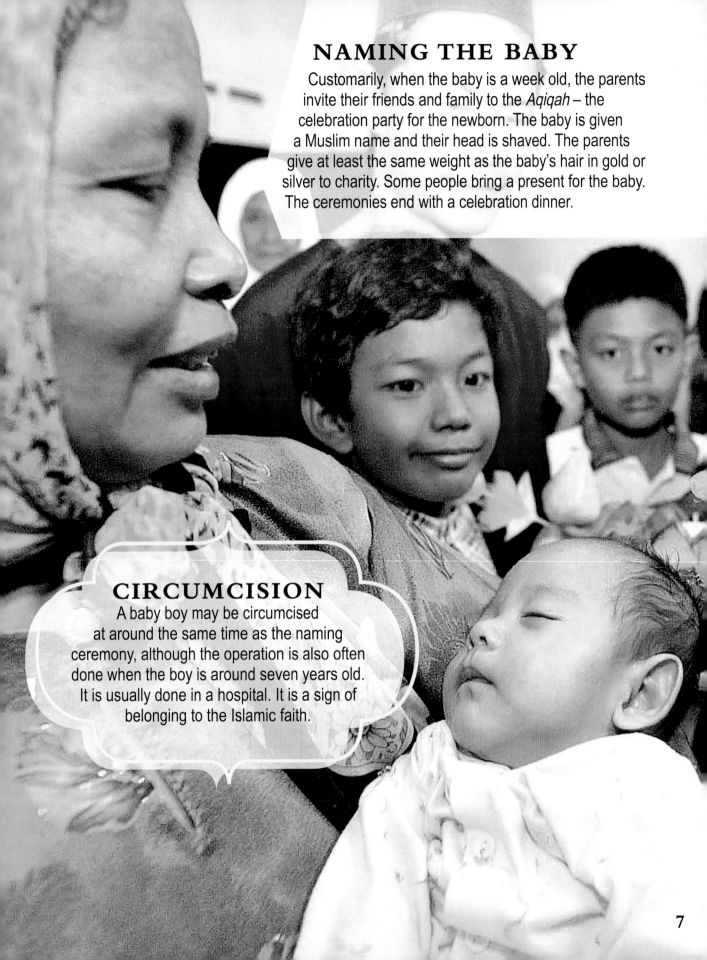

NAMING THE BABY

Customarily, when the baby is a week old, the parents invite their friends and family to the *Aqiqah* – the celebration party for the newborn. The baby is given a Muslim name and their head is shaved. The parents give at least the same weight as the baby's hair in gold or silver to charity. Some people bring a present for the baby. The ceremonies end with a celebration dinner.

CIRCUMCISION

A baby boy may be circumcised at around the same time as the naming ceremony, although the operation is also often done when the boy is around seven years old. It is usually done in a hospital. It is a sign of belonging to the Islamic faith.

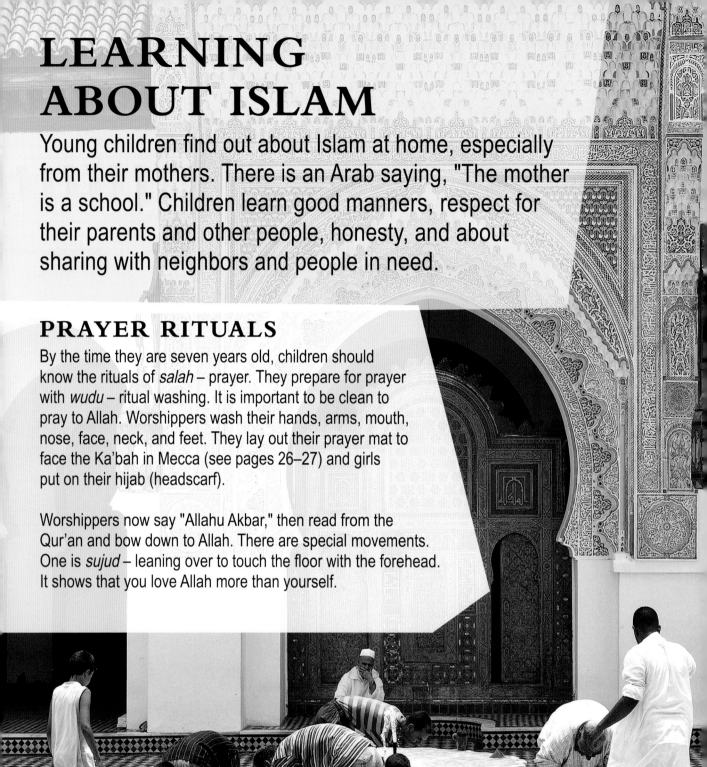

LEARNING ABOUT ISLAM

Young children find out about Islam at home, especially from their mothers. There is an Arab saying, "The mother is a school." Children learn good manners, respect for their parents and other people, honesty, and about sharing with neighbors and people in need.

PRAYER RITUALS

By the time they are seven years old, children should know the rituals of *salah* – prayer. They prepare for prayer with *wudu* – ritual washing. It is important to be clean to pray to Allah. Worshippers wash their hands, arms, mouth, nose, face, neck, and feet. They lay out their prayer mat to face the Ka'bah in Mecca (see pages 26–27) and girls put on their hijab (headscarf).

Worshippers now say "Allahu Akbar," then read from the Qur'an and bow down to Allah. There are special movements. One is *sujud* – leaning over to touch the floor with the forehead. It shows that you love Allah more than yourself.

RULES

At the mosque, children learn about the Five Pillars of Islam – the main rules of their faith (see right). Once they are teenagers, they will follow the Pillars themselves. At schools and colleges, there is often a room where Muslims can pray.

The statement of faith:
« There is no God but Allah, and Muhammad is the Messenger of Allah.
« Pray five times a day.
« Give *zakah* – a tax on wealth.
« Fast during the month of Ramadan.
« Go on Hajj (pilgrimage) to Mecca once in a lifetime, if possible.

At home, the father leads the family in prayer. The mother leads prayers if he is not there.

Muslims face the holy city of Mecca in Saudi Arabia when they pray.

FOLLOWING THE QUR'AN

Children start studying the Qur'an from an early age. The Qur'an is written in Arabic and must be recited in this language. As well as the words, the sounds and rhythm of Allah's messages are important.

ISLAMIC SCHOOL

Children learn to read the Qur'an at classes at the mosque or *madrasah* – Islamic school. They are taught how to read Arabic. Over time, they read the entire Qur'an and memorize it.

FIRST LESSON

In India, the Bismillah ceremony takes place when children start to study the Qur'an, at age four. Family and friends visit the family home, and the father teaches the child their first lesson. To celebrate, everyone eats cake.

WHAT THE QUR'AN MEANS

Young people discover the meaning of the Qur'an by studying it in their own language. It gives guidance on Islamic beliefs, laws, and customs, as well as all aspects of daily life. At home, being a good Muslim means helping out – from clearing the table to caring for younger brothers and sisters. In the wider world, it means treating other people well, whether or not they share your faith. For Muslims, it is all part of learning how to respect Allah and the world he created.

CLOTHING

It is a Muslim custom for everybody – boys, girls, men, and women – to wear modest, loose-fitting clothes. When Muslim girls become teenagers, many start to wear a hijab when they go out. According to Islamic custom, a woman's hair is part of her beauty, so she should cover her head in public as a symbol of respect for herself and Allah. It is also a sign that she is proud of her religion.

FOOD AND MEALTIMES

The Qur'an has advice for all aspects of life, including mealtimes. Traditionally, Muslims from the Middle East eat dishes such as meat, rice, and vegetables from one large plate, helping themselves from the part nearest to them with their right hand. While they enjoy their meals, they try to follow the example of the Prophet Muhammad not to rush their meal or eat too much!

HALAL

Islam teaches that some foods are good for you and some are harmful. Food Muslims can consume is *halal* – permitted. They may eat halal meat, which comes from plant-eating animals, such as cows and sheep. The animals must be farmed and killed in a humane way, though, according to *Shari'ah* – Muslim law. Muslims may eat eggs from halal birds and any fruit and vegetables they like. The rules do not stop them from eating common Western foods, such as burgers and fries. But many Muslims check the ingredients of processed foods carefully to make sure they are halal.

HARAM

Food that Muslims must not eat is *haram* –
forbidden. They never eat meat from animals
that feed on other creatures or any meat from
pigs, and some will not consume shellfish.
Horses, mules, and donkeys are not usually
eaten in Muslim countries either. Muslims never
drink alcohol. To them, all drugs not prescribed
by a doctor are devices of Satan – the devil.
They lead people to escape from real life, which
means they cannot serve Allah as they should.
Serving Allah includes offering food to others,
especially at family and religious celebrations.
At festivals, Muslims cook many delicious
dishes and share them with their Muslim and
non-Muslim neighbors.

DON'T OVEREAT!

The Prophet Muhammad
taught that it is best for the stomach
to be one-third full of food,
one-third full with water
and one-third empty.

GOING TO THE MOSQUE

Muslims practice their faith at home, but they also go to the mosque for worship, study, and social occasions. It is the center of their community. Women sometimes pray at home rather than at the mosque, but they attend it for classes and events.

Mosque in Iran

SIMILARITIES AND DIFFERENCES

Mosques vary enormously. In West Africa, they may be sand-colored, mud-brick structures. In Iran and Turkey, brightly colored tiles often cover the walls, while in Arab countries, many mosques are painted white.

All have a minaret – a tower where, in Muslim countries, a man called the *muezzin* calls the faithful to prayer. Inside is a *mihrab*, a niche with a sign indicating the *qiblah*, the direction of Mecca. The imam stands at a platform called the *minbar* to talk to the worshippers. Mosques often have a prayer area for men and a separate one for women and children. Large mosques have an open courtyard for gatherings.

Mosque in West Africa

FRIDAY PRAYERS

The biggest weekly gathering is for Friday midday prayers. If they can, men stop what they are doing and head to the mosque. They remove their shoes to keep their place of worship clean, and perform *wudu* to cleanse themselves before entering. The mosque soon becomes crowded, with worshippers tightly packed into the prayer hall in neat rows.

The imam gives a talk from the Qur'an, tells a story about the Prophet Muhammad, or talks about how to apply Islam to daily life. The worshippers then say prayers. Going to the mosque helps people feel closer to Allah.

Women and girls wear a hijab to visit the mosque. They may also wear a garment called a burka that covers them from head to foot. Men often wear a long white robe and prayer hat.

THE IMAM

The imam is an important and respected member of the Islamic community. He leads the five daily prayers at the mosque and carries out religious ceremonies. He gives advice on Islamic customs and dealing with problems based on the teachings of the Qur'an. Outside the mosque, he visits elderly and sick people in the community. An imam has to be a man to lead men in prayer, but a group of women may choose a woman to lead their prayers.

FASTING AT RAMADAN

Muslims visit the mosque frequently during the ninth month of the Islamic year – Ramadan. It is the month of fasting and a time for renewing faith. By not thinking about basic matters like food, people have more time to pray and focus on their spiritual life. Fasting teaches Muslims self-control and reminds them about people who go hungry.

The suhur meal keeps everyone going until they break the fast the following evening.

TAKING PART

During Ramadan, no food or drink may pass people's lips between sunrise and sunset each day. All healthy Muslims over the age of 12 take part. Pregnant women and those who are ill do not fast, though. It can be difficult for children at first, but it is not dangerous because they eat well in the evening and before dawn. They often find it exciting getting up in the night for *suhur*, the early breakfast before sunrise. Fasting can help them to feel part of their community and often brings a sense of achievement.

BREAKING THE FAST

People break the fast after the sunset prayers. It is traditional to eat a few dates with some water, but the customs vary. In Turkey, the fast is broken with olives and tea. In India, it is broken with a sweet milky drink and some fruit. Men often go to the mosque for sunset prayers. Afterwards, families enjoy a nourishing main meal, *iftar*, to fill them up. Meat with rice and yogurt are common dishes. In Morocco, people eat a thick soup called *harira*, with lentils and chickpeas, followed by sweet mint tea, dates, or almond cakes.

During Ramadan, Muslims spend time reading the Qur'an. They focus on forgiving anyone who has upset them, and try to give up bad habits to become better people.

Moroccan
harira soup

THE MUSLIM CALENDAR

Muslims follow a lunar calendar. Each month starts with the new moon and is 29 or 30 days long. The Muslim year is about 11 days shorter than the solar year, so the months do not stay in the same seasons. This means Ramadan can happen during any season.

It gives a great sense of community to know that Muslims around the world are taking part in Ramadan at the same time.

CARING FOR THE COMMUNITY

During Ramadan, people focus their thoughts on helping others. Before the end of the month, Muslims make sure everyone in the community will be able to celebrate Eid al-Fitr (see pages 20–21) by giving zakah at the mosque. The mosque gives out the money to poor people. Eid is a time for being especially kind to others.

RUNNING THE MOSQUE

People do not only help others at Ramadan. Throughout the year, a management committee elected by members of the mosque share the work of running it. The members meet every week for prayers and a *khutbah* (sermon). They discuss any problems – for example, how to help someone in their community who is in poverty, or solve a dispute. They try to support each other the best they can. The group also helps to organize education about the Qur'an and Islamic teaching for people of all ages and collects zakah.

ALLAH WILL SEE

Muslims believe that Allah will reward people for good deeds: "Those who believe, and do deeds of righteousness, and establish regular prayers and regular charity, will have their reward with their Lord: on them shall be no fear nor shall they grieve." (Al Baqarah: Ayat 277)

CARING AND SHARING

It is also a Muslim duty to donate money throughout the year. People give *sadaqah* – voluntary contributions to charity. In the UK, Muslims are the most generous givers to charity of any religious community. There are plenty of Muslim charities to support, including Red Crescent, Islamic Relief Worldwide, and Muslim Aid.

These large charities work around the world. Islamic Relief helps survivors of disasters, runs programs to assist orphans, and creates business opportunities for those in poverty. The Pakistan Red Crescent Society works in communities, training thousands of youth volunteers to help out in emergencies. Whether they donate to charity or take part in community work themselves, Muslims are all contributing to the ummah.

People give zakah at the mosque – a religious tax that allows richer members of the community to help those who are less well off.

EID AL-FITR

The feast after Ramadan is one of the major Muslim festivals. It is a joyful festival to thank Allah for the strength to fast and for the gift of the Qur'an. In Muslim countries, such as Indonesia and Pakistan, Eid al-Fitr is a national holiday. In other countries, Muslims simply take the day off work and school.

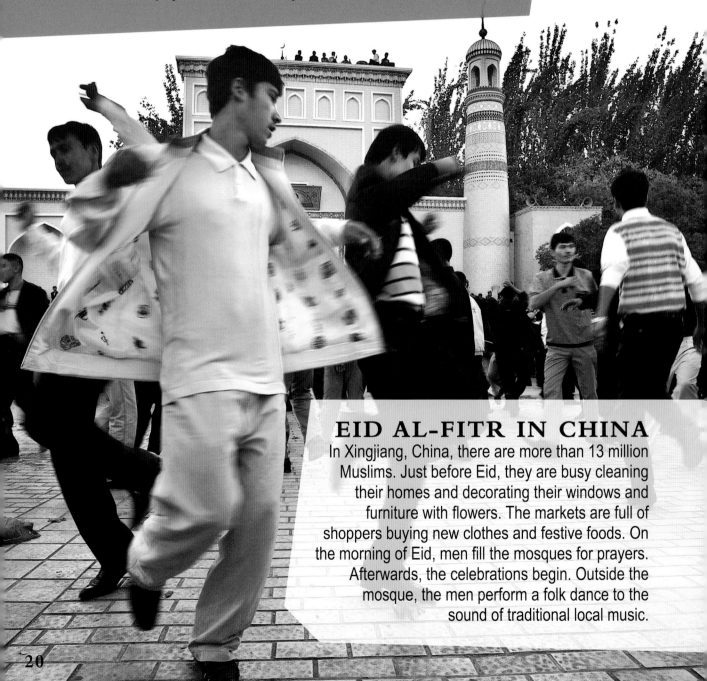

EID AL-FITR IN CHINA

In Xingjiang, China, there are more than 13 million Muslims. Just before Eid, they are busy cleaning their homes and decorating their windows and furniture with flowers. The markets are full of shoppers buying new clothes and festive foods. On the morning of Eid, men fill the mosques for prayers. Afterwards, the celebrations begin. Outside the mosque, the men perform a folk dance to the sound of traditional local music.

HAPPY EID

In the last couple of days of Ramadan, people look out for the new moon, the sign the next month is beginning. The following day is Eid. It is an exciting day. Everyone says their morning prayers and dresses in their best clothes, and they wish each other "*Eid Mubarak*" – Happy Eid. Children make cards and may hang up decorations to create a festive atmosphere. Parents give their children clothes and gifts or money so they become even more excited!

Men go to special prayers at the mosque. Some women and girls go, too, but pray separately. The imam gives a talk about how to become a better Muslim.

EID FEAST

After prayers, families hold a festive meal with friends and family, enjoying rich foods, sweets, and cakes. For older children and adults, it is the first meal they have eaten in daylight for a month. They take portions of their feast to share with their neighbors and visit others to wish them a happy Eid.

Eid dishes and colorful decorations

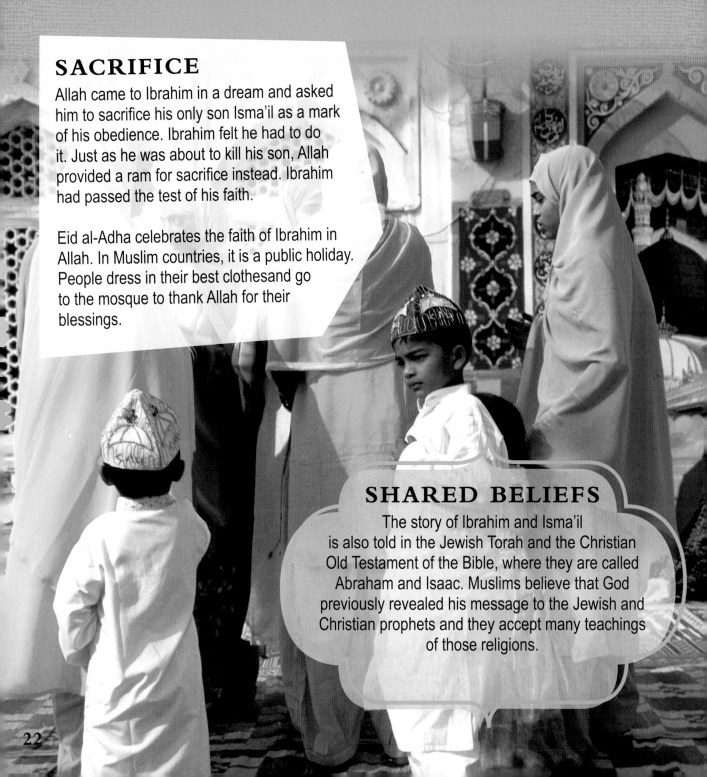

EID AL-ADHA

The second major festival of Islam is Eid al-Adha, which follows the Hajj (see pages 26–27). It means Feast of the Sacrifice. The Qur'an tells the story.

SACRIFICE

Allah came to Ibrahim in a dream and asked him to sacrifice his only son Isma'il as a mark of his obedience. Ibrahim felt he had to do it. Just as he was about to kill his son, Allah provided a ram for sacrifice instead. Ibrahim had passed the test of his faith.

Eid al-Adha celebrates the faith of Ibrahim in Allah. In Muslim countries, it is a public holiday. People dress in their best clothesand go to the mosque to thank Allah for their blessings.

SHARED BELIEFS

The story of Ibrahim and Isma'il is also told in the Jewish Torah and the Christian Old Testament of the Bible, where they are called Abraham and Isaac. Muslims believe that God previously revealed his message to the Jewish and Christian prophets and they accept many teachings of those religions.

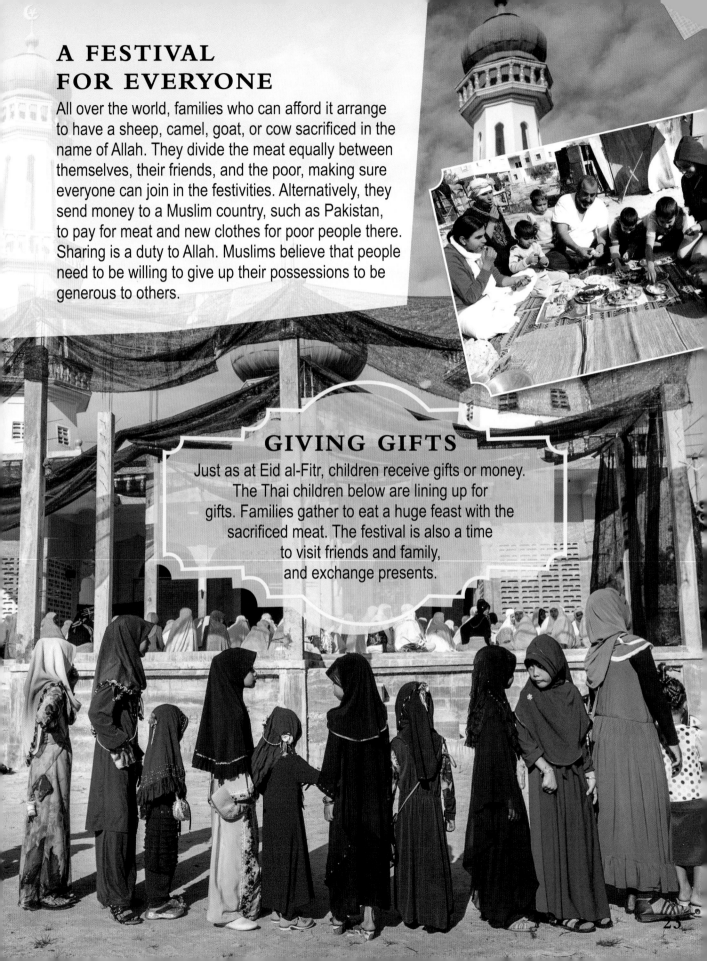

A FESTIVAL FOR EVERYONE

All over the world, families who can afford it arrange to have a sheep, camel, goat, or cow sacrificed in the name of Allah. They divide the meat equally between themselves, their friends, and the poor, making sure everyone can join in the festivities. Alternatively, they send money to a Muslim country, such as Pakistan, to pay for meat and new clothes for poor people there. Sharing is a duty to Allah. Muslims believe that people need to be willing to give up their possessions to be generous to others.

GIVING GIFTS

Just as at Eid al-Fitr, children receive gifts or money. The Thai children below are lining up for gifts. Families gather to eat a huge feast with the sacrificed meat. The festival is also a time to visit friends and family, and exchange presents.

A MUSLIM WEDDING

As well as religious festivals, Muslims hold family celebrations – including weddings. Parents often help their adult children to find a partner, but the young people make the final decision about whom to marry themselves.

PRE-WEDDING RITUALS

Once a couple agree to marry, they hold an engagement party and may exchange gold rings to show their commitment. For many brides, the night before her wedding is Henna Night. Female friends and relatives decorate her hands and feet with beautiful henna patterns. The following morning, the bride and groom dress in their finest clothes for the ceremony.

WEDDING CEREMONY

Muslims often marry at the mosque, but they can hold the wedding at home or elsewhere, too. Often the imam carries out the ceremony, although any Muslim man can marry the couple. The pair make their own legal contract (agreement). The groom gives a sum of money to the bride and promises to look after her, and she keeps any property or money of her own.

At the wedding, the bride and groom sit in different rooms or at opposite sides of the same room. The witnesses hear them say their vows. The ceremony leader reads from the Qur'an and talks about the duties within marriage. He asks each person three times if they agree to be married, then they sign the wedding contract.

The groom's family presents a feast called a walimah – marriage banquet.

WHEN MARRIAGE GOES WRONG

Divorce is allowed in Islam if the couple are truly unhappy, but only as a last resort. They try for three months to resolve their problems. Only if this fails do the couple then divorce.

GOING ON HAJJ

Another special lifetime event is the pilgrimage to the holy places in Saudi Arabia. Each year, about three million Muslims go on Hajj. It is one of the largest gatherings of people in the world.

MECCA

Mecca is the holiest site in Islam because the Prophet Muhammad received his first messages from Allah here. To enter the holy city, pilgrims change into simple, unsewn white robes called *ihram* – a symbol that all are equal in Allah's eyes.

The Hajj rituals mark significant events in the lives of the Prophets Ibrahim, Isma'il, and Muhammad.

Muslim pilgrims "stone the devil" at the Jamarat pillars in Mina, outside Mecca.

HAJJ RITUALS

• Circling the Ka'bah seven times; the first monument built for the worship of Allah.
• Praying for Allah's forgiveness at Mount Arafat, where Muhammad gave his final sermon.
• Throwing stones at the Jamarat pillars that stand for the devil and bad actions.
• Drinking from the well of Zamzam, where water appeared for Hajar, the wife of Ibrahim.
• Running seven times between the hills of Safa and Marwah, as Hajar did, seeking water for her baby son Isma'il.

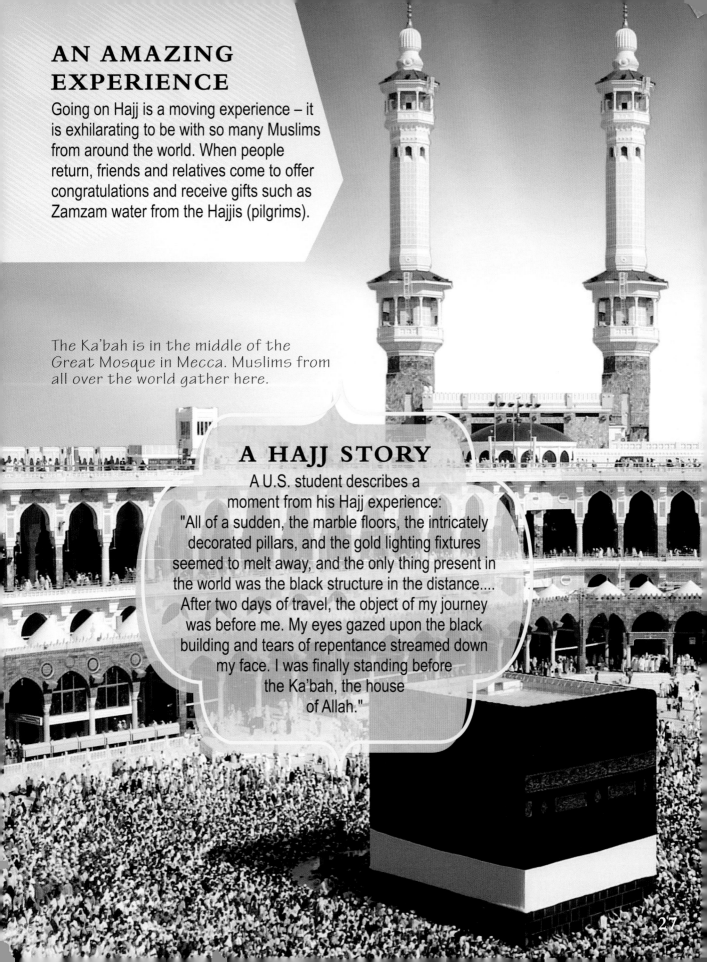

AN AMAZING EXPERIENCE

Going on Hajj is a moving experience – it is exhilarating to be with so many Muslims from around the world. When people return, friends and relatives come to offer congratulations and receive gifts such as Zamzam water from the Hajjis (pilgrims).

The Ka'bah is in the middle of the Great Mosque in Mecca. Muslims from all over the world gather here.

A HAJJ STORY

A U.S. student describes a moment from his Hajj experience:
"All of a sudden, the marble floors, the intricately decorated pillars, and the gold lighting fixtures seemed to melt away, and the only thing present in the world was the black structure in the distance.... After two days of travel, the object of my journey was before me. My eyes gazed upon the black building and tears of repentance streamed down my face. I was finally standing before the Ka'bah, the house of Allah."

LIFE'S END

As rituals help Muslims to maintain their faith throughout their lives, they also help them prepare for death. Their faith is a source of strength. Death is part of Allah's will and Muslims accept it. When they know they are dying, they try to say the *shahadah*, the statement of faith in Allah: "There is no God but Allah, and Muhammad is the messenger of Allah." Muslims believe they will be with Allah after death. When people hear of a death, they say "To Allah we belong and to Him is our return." (Qur'an 2:156)

PARADISE

Muslims believe that people who behave well in life and are good to others will go to Paradise (heaven): "People who have faith and do righteous [good] deeds are the best of creatures. Their reward is with Allah: they will live forever in Gardens of Eternity (paradise)."
(Surah 98: 7–8)

IMPORTANT RITUALS

A close friend or relative prepares the body for burial, washing it thoroughly and dressing it in plain clothes. A man is shrouded in three pieces of white cloth, a woman in five. If the person has been on Hajj, they are dressed in their pilgrimage robes. The body is taken to the mosque and the mourners gather for funeral prayers. Muslims bury their dead within 24 hours if they can. They are never cremated (burned).

The imam leads the prayers at a funeral in Malaysia.

PRAYERS, FOOD, AND COMFORT

After the death of a loved one, the family stays at home reading the Qur'an for between three and seven days, depending on local customs. Passages in the holy book comfort the grieving family. Friends and relatives bring meals and offer their support. At festivals, the family remember the person who passed away and visit their grave to show respect.

Visiting a grave to pray and remember a loved one

GLOSSARY

call to prayer The call from the mosque to let people know it is time for prayer

fast To go without food for religious reasons

halal Meat from an animal that has been killed and prepared according to Islamic law

haram Not permitted by Islamic law

henna A red dye that is used to change the color of the skin for a short time

hijab A headscarf that many Muslim girls and women wear to cover their hair, as a sign of modesty

Eid A Muslim holiday

iftar The meal Muslims eat after sunset during Ramadan

imam A person who leads the prayers in the mosque and is a leader in the Muslim community

Ka'bah The building in the center of the Great Mosque in Mecca, the site that is most holy to Muslims; Muslims face the Ka'bah when they pray

khutbah A religious sermon, or talk, by the imam in the mosque, such as at Friday prayers and Eid

Mecca The holy city in Saudi Arabia where the Prophet Muhammad was born and where he started to teach his message

Middle East An area that covers Southwest Asia and includes countries such as Egypt, Iraq, Iran, and Saudi Arabia.

mosque The Muslim place of worship

pilgrimage A journey to a holy place for religious reasons

prophet In Islam, a person sent by Allah to teach the people and give them messages from Allah

Qur'an The Muslim holy book, written in 114 chapters called surahs

rite of passage A ceremony or an event that marks an important stage in somebody's life

ritual A set of actions done in the same way each time, for example during a religious ceremony

sacrifice To kill an animal to offer to Allah

sadaqah Voluntary giving to charity of any amount at any time of year

salah The Muslim religious duty to pray to Allah five times a day

shahadah The Muslim statement of faith: "There is no god but Allah, and Muhammad is the messenger of Allah"

solar year The time it takes for Earth to complete one orbit of the sun; 365 days, 5 hours, 48 minutes, and 46 seconds

spiritual To do with the human mind and feelings, rather than the body, and often used to describe religious feelings

suhur The meal Muslims eat just before dawn during Ramadan

ummah The community of Muslims in the world

wudu Ritual washing that Muslims carry out so they are clean for prayer

zakah Giving money to charity as a religious duty. Each year Muslims give 2.5 percent of their income and savings after they have taken care of their families. The poorest people do not pay it.

FIND OUT MORE

Books

Guillain, Charlotte. *Islamic Culture*. Chicago, IL: Heinemann Library, 2013.

Murray, Julie. *Ramadan*. Minneapolis, MN: Abdo Kids, 2018.

Syed, Tayyaba. *Islam*. New York, NY: Britannica Educational Publishing, 2019.

Websites
BBC Religions Islam
www.bbc.co.uk/religion/religions/islam/
This website offers a good general introduction to many aspects of Islam.

Early Islamic World: Islam
www.ducksters.com/history/islam/islam.php
Learn more about Islam here.

Ramadan
www.dkfindout.com/us/more-find-out/festivals-and-holidays/ramadan
Read more about Ramadan on this page.

Note to parents and teachers:
Every effort has been made by the publishers to ensure that the websites in this book are suitable for children, that they are of the highest educational value, and that they contain no inappropriate or offensive material. However, because of the nature of the Internet, it is impossible to guarantee that the contents of these sites will not be altered. We strongly advise that Internet access is supervised by a responsible adult.

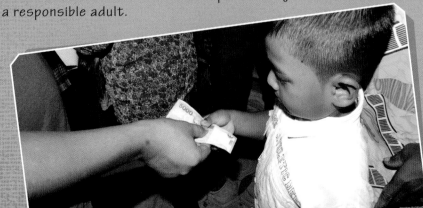

INDEX